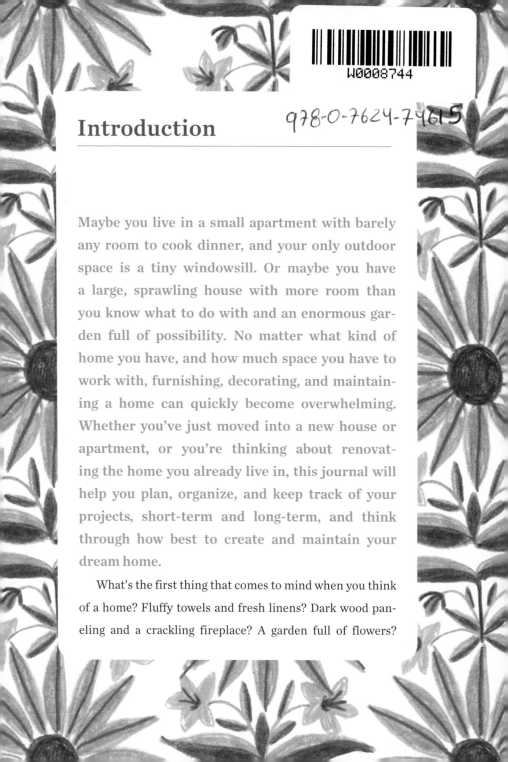

Introduction

978-0-7624-7615

W0008744

Maybe you live in a small apartment with barely any room to cook dinner, and your only outdoor space is a tiny windowsill. Or maybe you have a large, sprawling house with more room than you know what to do with and an enormous garden full of possibility. No matter what kind of home you have, and how much space you have to work with, furnishing, decorating, and maintaining a home can quickly become overwhelming. Whether you've just moved into a new house or apartment, or you're thinking about renovating the home you already live in, this journal will help you plan, organize, and keep track of your projects, short-term and long-term, and think through how best to create and maintain your dream home.

What's the first thing that comes to mind when you think of a home? Fluffy towels and fresh linens? Dark wood paneling and a crackling fireplace? A garden full of flowers?

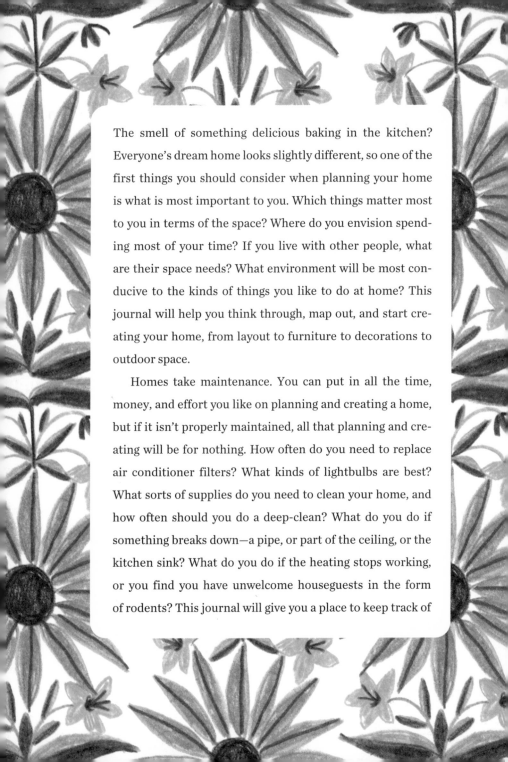

The smell of something delicious baking in the kitchen? Everyone's dream home looks slightly different, so one of the first things you should consider when planning your home is what is most important to you. Which things matter most to you in terms of the space? Where do you envision spending most of your time? If you live with other people, what are their space needs? What environment will be most conducive to the kinds of things you like to do at home? This journal will help you think through, map out, and start creating your home, from layout to furniture to decorations to outdoor space.

Homes take maintenance. You can put in all the time, money, and effort you like on planning and creating a home, but if it isn't properly maintained, all that planning and creating will be for nothing. How often do you need to replace air conditioner filters? What kinds of lightbulbs are best? What sorts of supplies do you need to clean your home, and how often should you do a deep-clean? What do you do if something breaks down—a pipe, or part of the ceiling, or the kitchen sink? What do you do if the heating stops working, or you find you have unwelcome houseguests in the form of rodents? This journal will give you a place to keep track of home improvements and renovations, and store names and numbers of professionals to call when something goes wrong.

You're probably never going to be able to make your home into *everything* you've ever wanted, but there's no reason you can't dream—and there's no reason that many of those dreams can't eventually come true. Is there some piece of furniture or art you've always wanted? Are there organizational tools or filing solutions you've dreamed of but haven't been able to put into place? Have you always wanted a built-in bookcase, or a certain kind of fruit tree, or a stained-glass window in your kitchen? Everyone's dreams are different, and some of them may be too expensive or time-consuming or difficult to make happen. But maybe some of them are achievable, either now or in the future, and maybe there are smaller steps you can take to work toward them. This journal will let you record any dreams you have for your home and brainstorm steps you can take now to get closer to them.

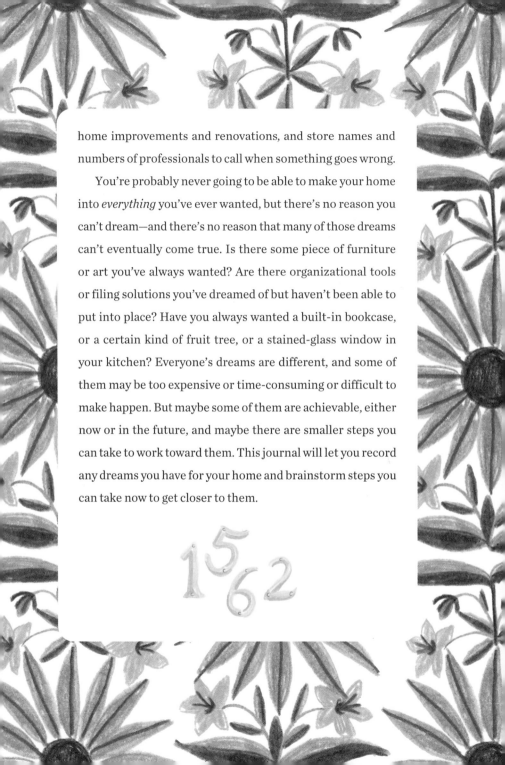

PLANNING
& CREATING

When you're planning your home, you need to consider which things are most important to you. Picture yourself in your new home or think about yourself in your current one. Where do you spend your time? How do you envision yourself fitting into the space? These things will determine how you lay out your home, and what kind of furniture and decorations you need.

Consider some of the following questions to start thinking about how to lay out your home:

Do you need large seating areas?

_____

_____

_____

_____

_____

Do you want a lot of out-of-sight storage, so your house is clutter-free?

_____

_____

_____

_____

_____

Do you like an environment with a lot of books and visible decorations, or do you prefer the decorations to be sparse?

_____

_____

_____

_____

_____

Do you work from home and/or need an office space?

_____

_____

_____

_____

_____

Do you spend a lot of time watching TV or listening to music?

_____

_____

_____

_____

_____

If you don't live alone, where do the other people you live with spend their time?

_____

_____

_____

_____

_____

Does everyone you live with need their own space, or do you all cluster together all the time?

_____

_____

_____

_____

_____

Do you need a big kitchen table because you spend a lot of time around there, or do you prefer to eat on the go?

_____

_____

_____

_____

_____

_____

Do you have very young children? Is there anything you need
to do to make your home safe for babies?

_____

_____

_____

_____

_____

Do you have any pets? Is there anything you need to do to
pet-proof your home?

_____

_____

_____

_____

_____

_____

Floorplan

How many rooms are there? Where are they in relation to one another? How many closets does each have? Measure all rooms and sketch out a floorplan on the pages that follow so you can see how much space you have and figure out where your furniture should go.

Based on how many rooms you have to work with, you might want to sketch out the whole house or apartment on one page, or you might want to look at each room separately. A good way to start is to measure the longest wall you have, count the number of squares on the long end of the graph paper (or the number of squares you want to use for that wall), and then divide the length of the wall by the number of squares to figure out how many feet (or meters, or other unit of measurement) each square is worth. For instance, if your wall is 60 feet and there are 30 squares across the page, then each square would be worth 2 feet. You can use the key you make to map out the rest of the walls and the other rooms.

KEY:

Kitchen

How large is the kitchen? Is there enough space for you to cook? Do you need to invest in a freestanding piece of furniture like a kitchen island that will give you extra counter space? Do you need to make room for a coffee maker or blender? Does everything work properly, or do you need to replace any key appliances? What do you absolutely need— things like a stove, a sink, a refrigerator—and what things would be nice but aren't absolutely necessary, like a freestanding ice maker or a single-serve coffee machine? These lists will be different for everyone; use the following planning pages to keep track of what you already have, what you need to get, and what you would like to have in an ideal world, as well as anything you can get rid of.

KITCHEN

WHAT DO I ALREADY HAVE THAT I PLAN TO KEEP?

☐ _____   ☐ _____
☐ _____   ☐ _____
☐ _____   ☐ _____
☐ _____   ☐ _____
☐ _____   ☐ _____
☐ _____   ☐ _____
☐ _____   ☐ _____
☐ _____   ☐ _____
☐ _____   ☐ _____
☐ _____   ☐ _____
☐ _____   ☐ _____
☐ _____   ☐ _____
☐ _____   ☐ _____
☐ _____   ☐ _____
☐ _____   ☐ _____
☐ _____   ☐ _____
☐ _____   ☐ _____
☐ _____   ☐ _____
☐ _____   ☐ _____
☐ _____   ☐ _____
☐ _____   ☐ _____
☐ _____   ☐ _____
☐ _____   ☐ _____

KITCHEN

WHAT DO I NEED TO GET?

- [ ] _____
- [ ] _____
- [ ] _____
- [ ] _____
- [ ] _____
- [ ] _____
- [ ] _____
- [ ] _____
- [ ] _____
- [ ] _____
- [ ] _____
- [ ] _____
- [ ] _____
- [ ] _____
- [ ] _____
- [ ] _____
- [ ] _____
- [ ] _____
- [ ] _____
- [ ] _____
- [ ] _____
- [ ] _____
- [ ] _____

- [ ] _____
- [ ] _____
- [ ] _____
- [ ] _____
- [ ] _____
- [ ] _____
- [ ] _____
- [ ] _____
- [ ] _____
- [ ] _____
- [ ] _____
- [ ] _____
- [ ] _____
- [ ] _____
- [ ] _____
- [ ] _____
- [ ] _____
- [ ] _____
- [ ] _____
- [ ] _____
- [ ] _____
- [ ] _____
- [ ] _____

KITCHEN

WHAT DO I WANT TO GET?

- [ ] _____
- [ ] _____
- [ ] _____
- [ ] _____
- [ ] _____
- [ ] _____
- [ ] _____
- [ ] _____
- [ ] _____
- [ ] _____
- [ ] _____
- [ ] _____
- [ ] _____
- [ ] _____
- [ ] _____
- [ ] _____
- [ ] _____
- [ ] _____
- [ ] _____
- [ ] _____
- [ ] _____
- [ ] _____
- [ ] _____
- [ ] _____

- [ ] _____
- [ ] _____
- [ ] _____
- [ ] _____
- [ ] _____
- [ ] _____
- [ ] _____
- [ ] _____
- [ ] _____
- [ ] _____
- [ ] _____
- [ ] _____
- [ ] _____
- [ ] _____
- [ ] _____
- [ ] _____
- [ ] _____
- [ ] _____
- [ ] _____
- [ ] _____
- [ ] _____
- [ ] _____
- [ ] _____
- [ ] _____

KITCHEN

WHAT DO I HAVE THAT I PLAN TO DONATE OR THROW AWAY?

ITEM	DONATE OR THROW AWAY?

Bedrooms

How many bedrooms are there? If you have kids or other people living with you, will they each have their own room or will they share? If there aren't enough bedrooms, is there a way to put up a temporary wall or a large bookcase or even a curtain to separate the space? You may also want to look into converting a smaller room or alcove into a bedroom, or lofting beds to create more space. For each bedroom, use the following planning pages to take stock of what furniture you already have, what you need, what you want, and what you can give away.

BEDROOM:

WHAT DO I ALREADY HAVE THAT I PLAN TO KEEP?

- [ ] _____
- [ ] _____
- [ ] _____
- [ ] _____
- [ ] _____
- [ ] _____
- [ ] _____
- [ ] _____
- [ ] _____
- [ ] _____
- [ ] _____
- [ ] _____
- [ ] _____
- [ ] _____
- [ ] _____
- [ ] _____
- [ ] _____
- [ ] _____
- [ ] _____
- [ ] _____
- [ ] _____
- [ ] _____
- [ ] _____
- [ ] _____

- [ ] _____
- [ ] _____
- [ ] _____
- [ ] _____
- [ ] _____
- [ ] _____
- [ ] _____
- [ ] _____
- [ ] _____
- [ ] _____
- [ ] _____
- [ ] _____
- [ ] _____
- [ ] _____
- [ ] _____
- [ ] _____
- [ ] _____
- [ ] _____
- [ ] _____
- [ ] _____
- [ ] _____
- [ ] _____
- [ ] _____

BEDROOM:

WHAT DO I NEED TO GET?

- [ ] _____
- [ ] _____
- [ ] _____
- [ ] _____
- [ ] _____
- [ ] _____
- [ ] _____
- [ ] _____
- [ ] _____
- [ ] _____
- [ ] _____
- [ ] _____
- [ ] _____
- [ ] _____
- [ ] _____
- [ ] _____
- [ ] _____
- [ ] _____
- [ ] _____
- [ ] _____
- [ ] _____
- [ ] _____
- [ ] _____
- [ ] _____

- [ ] _____
- [ ] _____
- [ ] _____
- [ ] _____
- [ ] _____
- [ ] _____
- [ ] _____
- [ ] _____
- [ ] _____
- [ ] _____
- [ ] _____
- [ ] _____
- [ ] _____
- [ ] _____
- [ ] _____
- [ ] _____
- [ ] _____
- [ ] _____
- [ ] _____
- [ ] _____
- [ ] _____
- [ ] _____
- [ ] _____
- [ ] _____

BEDROOM:

WHAT DO I WANT TO GET?

- [ ] _____
- [ ] _____
- [ ] _____
- [ ] _____
- [ ] _____
- [ ] _____
- [ ] _____
- [ ] _____
- [ ] _____
- [ ] _____
- [ ] _____
- [ ] _____
- [ ] _____
- [ ] _____
- [ ] _____
- [ ] _____
- [ ] _____
- [ ] _____
- [ ] _____
- [ ] _____
- [ ] _____
- [ ] _____
- [ ] _____
- [ ] _____
- [ ] _____

- [ ] _____
- [ ] _____
- [ ] _____
- [ ] _____
- [ ] _____
- [ ] _____
- [ ] _____
- [ ] _____
- [ ] _____
- [ ] _____
- [ ] _____
- [ ] _____
- [ ] _____
- [ ] _____
- [ ] _____
- [ ] _____
- [ ] _____
- [ ] _____
- [ ] _____
- [ ] _____
- [ ] _____
- [ ] _____
- [ ] _____
- [ ] _____
- [ ] _____

BEDROOM:

ITEM	DONATE OR THROW AWAY?

Bathrooms

Is there more than one bathroom? If you live with others, does everyone have their own bathroom, or do all or some of you share one? What items do you already have in your bathrooms, and what do you need? Do all of the major fixtures (toilets, tubs, sinks, etc.) work properly, or do you need to replace or fix anything? What about things like shower heads or cabinets? What about mirrors or the hooks on the back of the door? Use the following planning pages to record what basics you have (and what condition they're in), what you need to get, what you *want* to get, and what you can give up.

BATHROOM:

WHAT BASICS DO I HAVE, AND DO THEY REQUIRE REPAIRS OR REPLACEMENT?

ITEM	REPAIR? REPLACE? KEEP?

BATHROOM:

WHAT DO I NEED TO GET?

- [ ] _____
- [ ] _____
- [ ] _____
- [ ] _____
- [ ] _____
- [ ] _____
- [ ] _____
- [ ] _____
- [ ] _____
- [ ] _____
- [ ] _____
- [ ] _____
- [ ] _____
- [ ] _____
- [ ] _____
- [ ] _____
- [ ] _____
- [ ] _____
- [ ] _____
- [ ] _____
- [ ] _____
- [ ] _____
- [ ] _____

- [ ] _____
- [ ] _____
- [ ] _____
- [ ] _____
- [ ] _____
- [ ] _____
- [ ] _____
- [ ] _____
- [ ] _____
- [ ] _____
- [ ] _____
- [ ] _____
- [ ] _____
- [ ] _____
- [ ] _____
- [ ] _____
- [ ] _____
- [ ] _____
- [ ] _____
- [ ] _____
- [ ] _____
- [ ] _____
- [ ] _____

BATHROOM:

☐ _____   ☐ _____
☐ _____   ☐ _____
☐ _____   ☐ _____
☐ _____   ☐ _____
☐ _____   ☐ _____
☐ _____   ☐ _____
☐ _____   ☐ _____
☐ _____   ☐ _____
☐ _____   ☐ _____
☐ _____   ☐ _____
☐ _____   ☐ _____
☐ _____   ☐ _____
☐ _____   ☐ _____
☐ _____   ☐ _____
☐ _____   ☐ _____
☐ _____   ☐ _____
☐ _____   ☐ _____
☐ _____   ☐ _____
☐ _____   ☐ _____
☐ _____   ☐ _____
☐ _____   ☐ _____
☐ _____   ☐ _____

BATHROOM:

WHAT DO I HAVE THAT I PLAN TO DONATE OR THROW AWAY?

ITEM	DONATE OR THROW AWAY?

BATHROOM:

ITEM	REPAIR? REPLACE? KEEP?

BATHROOM:

WHAT DO I NEED TO GET?

☐ _____   ☐ _____
☐ _____   ☐ _____
☐ _____   ☐ _____
☐ _____   ☐ _____
☐ _____   ☐ _____
☐ _____   ☐ _____
☐ _____   ☐ _____
☐ _____   ☐ _____
☐ _____   ☐ _____
☐ _____   ☐ _____
☐ _____   ☐ _____
☐ _____   ☐ _____
☐ _____   ☐ _____
☐ _____   ☐ _____
☐ _____   ☐ _____
☐ _____   ☐ _____
☐ _____   ☐ _____
☐ _____   ☐ _____
☐ _____   ☐ _____
☐ _____   ☐ _____
☐ _____   ☐ _____
☐ _____   ☐ _____
☐ _____   ☐ _____
☐ _____   ☐ _____
☐ _____   ☐ _____

BATHROOM:

WHAT DO I WANT TO GET?

- [ ] _____
- [ ] _____
- [ ] _____
- [ ] _____
- [ ] _____
- [ ] _____
- [ ] _____
- [ ] _____
- [ ] _____
- [ ] _____
- [ ] _____
- [ ] _____
- [ ] _____
- [ ] _____
- [ ] _____
- [ ] _____
- [ ] _____
- [ ] _____
- [ ] _____
- [ ] _____
- [ ] _____
- [ ] _____
- [ ] _____

BATHROOM:

ITEM	DONATE OR THROW AWAY?

Living Room, Den, or Study

How many living areas do you have? How are you going to be using them? Do you need furniture like comfortable chairs and throw pillows for relaxing and socializing, or do you need a desk and bookshelves for working at home? Do you want a TV, and if so, do you need a TV stand? What about storage space for DVDs or records? How about bookshelves? Based on what you're going to be using your living areas for, use the following planning pages to record what kinds of furniture you have, what you need to get, what you can get rid of, and what things you'd like in an ideal world.

ROOM NAME:

WHAT DO I ALREADY HAVE THAT I PLAN TO KEEP?

- [ ] _____
- [ ] _____
- [ ] _____
- [ ] _____
- [ ] _____
- [ ] _____
- [ ] _____
- [ ] _____
- [ ] _____
- [ ] _____
- [ ] _____
- [ ] _____
- [ ] _____
- [ ] _____
- [ ] _____
- [ ] _____
- [ ] _____
- [ ] _____
- [ ] _____
- [ ] _____
- [ ] _____
- [ ] _____
- [ ] _____

- [ ] _____
- [ ] _____
- [ ] _____
- [ ] _____
- [ ] _____
- [ ] _____
- [ ] _____
- [ ] _____
- [ ] _____
- [ ] _____
- [ ] _____
- [ ] _____
- [ ] _____
- [ ] _____
- [ ] _____
- [ ] _____
- [ ] _____
- [ ] _____
- [ ] _____
- [ ] _____
- [ ] _____
- [ ] _____
- [ ] _____

ROOM NAME:

WHAT DO I NEED TO GET?

- [ ] _____
- [ ] _____
- [ ] _____
- [ ] _____
- [ ] _____
- [ ] _____
- [ ] _____
- [ ] _____
- [ ] _____
- [ ] _____
- [ ] _____
- [ ] _____
- [ ] _____
- [ ] _____
- [ ] _____
- [ ] _____
- [ ] _____
- [ ] _____
- [ ] _____
- [ ] _____
- [ ] _____
- [ ] _____

- [ ] _____
- [ ] _____
- [ ] _____
- [ ] _____
- [ ] _____
- [ ] _____
- [ ] _____
- [ ] _____
- [ ] _____
- [ ] _____
- [ ] _____
- [ ] _____
- [ ] _____
- [ ] _____
- [ ] _____
- [ ] _____
- [ ] _____
- [ ] _____
- [ ] _____
- [ ] _____
- [ ] _____
- [ ] _____

ROOM NAME:

WHAT DO I WANT TO GET?

- [ ] _____
- [ ] _____
- [ ] _____
- [ ] _____
- [ ] _____
- [ ] _____
- [ ] _____
- [ ] _____
- [ ] _____
- [ ] _____
- [ ] _____
- [ ] _____
- [ ] _____
- [ ] _____
- [ ] _____
- [ ] _____
- [ ] _____
- [ ] _____
- [ ] _____
- [ ] _____
- [ ] _____
- [ ] _____
- [ ] _____

- [ ] _____
- [ ] _____
- [ ] _____
- [ ] _____
- [ ] _____
- [ ] _____
- [ ] _____
- [ ] _____
- [ ] _____
- [ ] _____
- [ ] _____
- [ ] _____
- [ ] _____
- [ ] _____
- [ ] _____
- [ ] _____
- [ ] _____
- [ ] _____
- [ ] _____
- [ ] _____
- [ ] _____
- [ ] _____
- [ ] _____

ROOM NAME:

ITEM	DONATE OR THROW AWAY?

ROOM NAME:

WHAT DO I ALREADY HAVE THAT I PLAN TO KEEP?

- [ ] _____
- [ ] _____
- [ ] _____
- [ ] _____
- [ ] _____
- [ ] _____
- [ ] _____
- [ ] _____
- [ ] _____
- [ ] _____
- [ ] _____
- [ ] _____
- [ ] _____
- [ ] _____
- [ ] _____
- [ ] _____
- [ ] _____
- [ ] _____
- [ ] _____
- [ ] _____
- [ ] _____
- [ ] _____
- [ ] _____

- [ ] _____
- [ ] _____
- [ ] _____
- [ ] _____
- [ ] _____
- [ ] _____
- [ ] _____
- [ ] _____
- [ ] _____
- [ ] _____
- [ ] _____
- [ ] _____
- [ ] _____
- [ ] _____
- [ ] _____
- [ ] _____
- [ ] _____
- [ ] _____
- [ ] _____
- [ ] _____
- [ ] _____
- [ ] _____
- [ ] _____

ROOM NAME:

WHAT DO I NEED TO GET?

- [ ] _____
- [ ] _____
- [ ] _____
- [ ] _____
- [ ] _____
- [ ] _____
- [ ] _____
- [ ] _____
- [ ] _____
- [ ] _____
- [ ] _____
- [ ] _____
- [ ] _____
- [ ] _____
- [ ] _____
- [ ] _____
- [ ] _____
- [ ] _____
- [ ] _____
- [ ] _____
- [ ] _____
- [ ] _____
- [ ] _____

- [ ] _____
- [ ] _____
- [ ] _____
- [ ] _____
- [ ] _____
- [ ] _____
- [ ] _____
- [ ] _____
- [ ] _____
- [ ] _____
- [ ] _____
- [ ] _____
- [ ] _____
- [ ] _____
- [ ] _____
- [ ] _____
- [ ] _____
- [ ] _____
- [ ] _____
- [ ] _____
- [ ] _____
- [ ] _____
- [ ] _____

ROOM NAME:

☐ _____   ☐ _____
☐ _____   ☐ _____
☐ _____   ☐ _____
☐ _____   ☐ _____
☐ _____   ☐ _____
☐ _____   ☐ _____
☐ _____   ☐ _____
☐ _____   ☐ _____
☐ _____   ☐ _____
☐ _____   ☐ _____
☐ _____   ☐ _____
☐ _____   ☐ _____
☐ _____   ☐ _____
☐ _____   ☐ _____
☐ _____   ☐ _____
☐ _____   ☐ _____
☐ _____   ☐ _____
☐ _____   ☐ _____
☐ _____   ☐ _____
☐ _____   ☐ _____
☐ _____   ☐ _____
☐ _____   ☐ _____
☐ _____   ☐ _____
☐ _____   ☐ _____
☐ _____   ☐ _____

ROOM NAME:

WHAT DO I HAVE THAT I PLAN TO DONATE OR THROW AWAY?

ITEM	DONATE OR THROW AWAY?

Lighting

Lighting can make all the difference. It can make a small space seem larger, and it can make a large empty space feel homier and more inviting. What kind of lighting does each room in your home have? Overhead lighting? Lamps? Does your home get a lot of natural light? If not, you may want to supplement with more lamps, or you may want to choose a light color scheme for your walls and furniture to help brighten the space. You should also think through lampshades, which can make a big difference in what the light looks like, as well as lightbulbs. There are many lightbulb options; three of the most common are incandescent, fluorescent, and LED. They all have pros and cons, so you'll want to think through what's most important to you, whether that's cost, energy efficiency, quality of light, or lifespan. For instance, incandescent lightbulbs are relatively cheap and give off a nice warm light, but they aren't as energy efficient as LED bulbs. LEDs, on the other hand, are very energy efficient, last for a long time, and don't get hot to the touch, but they can have a less warm quality of light and are more expensive.

Consider how much light and what kind of light you would ideally have in each room, and brainstorm how to make it happen. Go through each room in your house and think through whether you have enough light, and whether you need or want to supplement with lamps or consider a different color scheme.

ROOM NAME	DESCRIPTION OF LIGHTING	ANY CHANGES?

Decorating

What is the overall aesthetic of your home now? How would you describe your home? What is your ideal aesthetic? What color schemes do you like? What style of furniture? What kinds of art or other decorations? Do you have or want houseplants? Do you have a lot of books or records or tchotchkes that you want displayed, or do you prefer to keep things like that out of sight? Go through every room in your house and record/brainstorm colors, art, and décor. This will let you see what you already have and what you still need, or, if you're starting fresh, it will help you figure out what you should acquire.

ROOM NAME	WALL COLOR, OTHER COLORS	STYLE OF FURNITURE

ROOM NAME	ART, OTHER DECORATIONS	RUGS, CARPETS

ROOM NAME	CURTAINS, BLINDS	PLANTS

Other Miscellaneous Items

Planning or renovating a home involves getting a lot of supplies and items you wouldn't necessarily think of at first, or might forget about— things like a router, or a printer, or hooks for hanging pictures. It can be helpful to jot down any items or appliances you think you may need, so that you have everything together in one place. It may turn out you don't need everything you thought you did, but it's a good idea to compile a list so that you don't forget anything essential.

Outdoors & Garden

Most people focus first on the inside of their home, but the outside is also important. Are there any improvements you want to make to the physical outside of your house, like painting or fixing the roof? If you live in a freestanding house, do you have a garden or a lawn? Flowerbeds? A porch? If you live in an apartment, do you have a balcony or fire escape? Windowsills? Are there any shrubs, flowers, herbs, or vegetables growing in your garden or on your balcony? Are there any you might want to introduce?

Consider some of the following questions:

If you live in a freestanding house, does the outside of the house need any major work? How's the roof? What material is the house made of? Does it need to be painted? Are the shingles in good shape? Do you need a new knocker, or a new coat of paint on the front/back doors? List any improvements that need to be made.

_____

_____

_____

_____

_____

_____

_____

_____

_____

_____

_____

How much space do you have outside? What are some ideas
you have for what to do with that space—for example, do you
want a grill, or an outdoor seating area? What steps would
you need to take to make that happen?

_____

_____

_____

_____

What's the climate like where you live? How much sunlight do you get? How much rainfall? What's the average temperature in each season? How dry or humid is your region?

_____

_____

_____

_____

_____

Do some research on what kinds of plants and flowers will grow in your area, and list some of the possibilities.

_____

_____

_____

_____

_____

What kinds of plants or flowers are you most excited to grow? Are there any herbs or vegetables that you can grow that would be useful for cooking?

_____

_____

_____

_____

_____

Do you have grass? Stones? Flowerbeds? What would you
have in an ideal world?

_____

_____

_____

_____

_____

	WHAT I HAVE	WHAT I WANT
VEGETABLES		
HERBS		
FLOWERS		
TREES		
OTHER PLANTS		

NOTES

• • •

• • •

NOTES

• • •

NOTES

• • •

NOTES

· · ·

NOTES

• • •

NOTES

NOTES

• • •

• • •

NOTES

- - -

. . .

NOTES

· · ·

NOTES

• • •

NOTES

・　・　・

· · ·

NOTES

• • •

· · ·

NOTES

• • •

NOTES

• • •

NOTES

NOTES

· · ·

NOTES

• • •

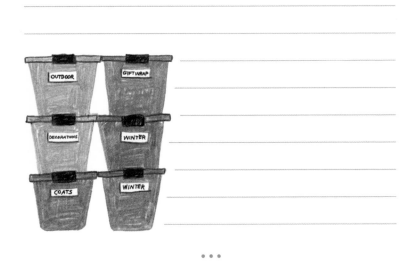

• • •

• • •

MAINTAINING

All homes need to be maintained, no matter how perfect they start out when they're new. Appliances break down, paint chips, and furniture starts to get worn. Sometimes it's possible to fix and touch things up as you go, and other times you'll need to do significant renovations or improvements. If you have to do any electrical work, or fix the plumbing, or install heating, or anything major like that, it may be easier—if possible—to take care of those things before you paint, fur-

nish, and decorate. If you're already living in your home and are planning to do some work on it, think through what you need to do the most, and what will be the least chaotic way to do those things. What should come first? What parts of your life will be disrupted while you're doing the renovation or making the improvements, and what steps can you take ahead of time to lessen the disruption?

It's useful to keep instruction manuals, warranty information, and receipts for all major appliances and pieces of furniture in one place (a physical drawer, for instance, or a folder in an online file storage system), so that you know where to look if anything breaks or if you need to get in touch with a manufacturer. It can also be helpful to keep track of how old certain appliances and items are, when they were last restored or fixed, and any major problems that have happened over the years.

Use the following checklist to keep track of major appliances (stove, refrigerator, freezer, dishwasher, etc.)

ITEM:	YEAR PURCHASED:
PROBLEMS:	WORK DONE, OTHER NOTES:

ITEM:	YEAR PURCHASED:
PROBLEMS:	WORK DONE, OTHER NOTES:

ITEM:	YEAR PURCHASED:
PROBLEMS:	WORK DONE, OTHER NOTES:

ITEM:	YEAR PURCHASED:
PROBLEMS:	WORK DONE, OTHER NOTES:

ITEM:	YEAR PURCHASED:
PROBLEMS:	WORK DONE, OTHER NOTES:

ITEM:	YEAR PURCHASED:
PROBLEMS:	WORK DONE, OTHER NOTES:

ITEM:	YEAR PURCHASED:
PROBLEMS:	WORK DONE, OTHER NOTES:

ITEM:	YEAR PURCHASED:
PROBLEMS:	WORK DONE, OTHER NOTES:

ITEM:	YEAR PURCHASED:
PROBLEMS:	WORK DONE, OTHER NOTES:

There are some things you can do yourself, but unless you're an electrician, for example, you probably won't be fixing wiring problems on your own. There are many databases of people who specialize in certain kinds of repair work, but it can also be helpful to keep a list of professionals you've hired yourself or professionals others have recommended to you. That way, if you have a rodent problem that you need to deal with right away, or a pipe bursts and you can't fix it yourself, you'll have a phone number ready to go.

NAME:	DATE OF SERVICE:
TYPE OF WORK:	DETAILS OF JOB:
PHONE #:	EMAIL:
QUALITY OF SERVICE: ☆ ☆ ☆ ☆ ☆	HIRE AGAIN? ☐ YES ☐ NO ☐ MAYBE

NAME:	DATE OF SERVICE:
TYPE OF WORK:	DETAILS OF JOB:
PHONE #:	EMAIL:
QUALITY OF SERVICE: ☆ ☆ ☆ ☆ ☆	HIRE AGAIN? ☐ YES ☐ NO ☐ MAYBE

NAME:	DATE OF SERVICE:
TYPE OF WORK:	DETAILS OF JOB:
PHONE #:	EMAIL:
QUALITY OF SERVICE: ☆ ☆ ☆ ☆ ☆	HIRE AGAIN? ☐ YES ☐ NO ☐ MAYBE

NAME:	DATE OF SERVICE:
TYPE OF WORK:	DETAILS OF JOB:
PHONE #:	EMAIL:
QUALITY OF SERVICE: ☆ ☆ ☆ ☆ ☆	HIRE AGAIN? ☐ YES ☐ NO ☐ MAYBE

NAME:	DATE OF SERVICE:
TYPE OF WORK:	DETAILS OF JOB:
PHONE #:	EMAIL:
QUALITY OF SERVICE: ☆ ☆ ☆ ☆ ☆	HIRE AGAIN? ☐ YES ☐ NO ☐ MAYBE

NAME:	DATE OF SERVICE:
TYPE OF WORK:	DETAILS OF JOB:
PHONE #:	EMAIL:
QUALITY OF SERVICE: ☆ ☆ ☆ ☆ ☆	HIRE AGAIN? ☐ YES ☐ NO ☐ MAYBE

NAME:	DATE OF SERVICE:
TYPE OF WORK:	DETAILS OF JOB:
PHONE #:	EMAIL:
QUALITY OF SERVICE: ☆ ☆ ☆ ☆ ☆	HIRE AGAIN? ☐ YES ☐ NO ☐ MAYBE

NAME:	DATE OF SERVICE:
TYPE OF WORK:	DETAILS OF JOB:
PHONE #:	EMAIL:
QUALITY OF SERVICE: ☆ ☆ ☆ ☆ ☆	HIRE AGAIN? ☐ YES ☐ NO ☐ MAYBE

NAME:	DATE OF SERVICE:
TYPE OF WORK:	DETAILS OF JOB:
PHONE #:	EMAIL:
QUALITY OF SERVICE: ☆ ☆ ☆ ☆ ☆	HIRE AGAIN? ☐ YES ☐ NO ☐ MAYBE

NAME:	DATE OF SERVICE:
TYPE OF WORK:	DETAILS OF JOB:
PHONE #:	EMAIL:
QUALITY OF SERVICE: ☆ ☆ ☆ ☆ ☆	HIRE AGAIN? ☐ YES ☐ NO ☐ MAYBE

NAME:	DATE OF SERVICE:
TYPE OF WORK:	DETAILS OF JOB:
PHONE #:	EMAIL:
QUALITY OF SERVICE: ☆ ☆ ☆ ☆ ☆	HIRE AGAIN? ☐ YES ☐ NO ☐ MAYBE

NAME:	DATE OF SERVICE:
TYPE OF WORK:	DETAILS OF JOB:
PHONE #:	EMAIL:
QUALITY OF SERVICE: ☆ ☆ ☆ ☆ ☆	HIRE AGAIN? ☐ YES ☐ NO ☐ MAYBE

It's also important to figure out how you're going to keep your home clean and organized. If you live with other people, who is responsible for which chores? This might be a good opportunity for you to revisit the distribution of chores in your household and make sure the burden isn't falling all on one person. Make a list of all the regular and ongoing household tasks you have to do—things like taking out the garbage, doing laundry, cooking dinner, washing dishes, vacuuming—and think through ways of splitting up the work so that no one is overwhelmed. You might even try making up a schedule so that everyone is on the same page.

If you live by yourself, it might help to spread out some of the work over the course of a week or a month so you don't get overwhelmed. For instance, you could plan to devote some small amount of time every day to cleaning, or you could choose to set aside a large chunk of just one day, maybe on the weekend, to get everything done. Likewise with cooking—you might prefer to cook simple, easy meals every day, or you might want to prepare a lot of food on one day that can be frozen or used throughout the week.

Try plotting out chores for a sample week by listing tasks you plan to do once a week or more—things like cooking, taking out the garbage, vacuuming—and then marking off which days you'll plan to complete those tasks. Play around with different approaches until you find the one that's the least stressful.

ROOM	MONDAY	TUESDAY	WEDNESDAY

THURSDAY	FRIDAY	SATURDAY	SUNDAY

Another way to plan is to list all the tasks you have to do on a weekly or monthly basis and plot out how many times per week/month you plan to do those things, and on what days.

WEEK #	MONDAY	TUESDAY	WEDNESDAY

Use the sample calendar below to try sketching out how often certain tasks need to be done and which days in general are best for completing them.

THURSDAY	FRIDAY	SATURDAY / SUNDAY

And then there are the tasks that you only have to do once, or a few times, every year. Think of those things—like cleaning your window screens or mulching your flower beds—and record them in the chart below.

TASK	MONTH(S)

TASK	MONTH(S)

TASK	MONTH(S)

TASK	MONTH(S)

It can also be helpful to keep track of specific cleaning and maintenance products—a specific brand of wood cleaner, certain kinds of alcohol wipes—that have worked especially well (or especially badly) so you know what to buy in the future. You may also want to include items you've read or heard about that you want to consider trying.

ITEM	BRAND	NOTES

ITEM	BRAND	NOTES

ITEM	BRAND	NOTES

ITEM	BRAND	NOTES

• • •

• • •

• • •

NOTES

...

• • •

• • •

• • •

NOTES

• • •

NOTES

NOTES

• • •

NOTES

· · ·

NOTES

• • •

NOTES

• • •

• • •

• • •

• • •

NOTES

. . .

• • •

NOTES

• • •

• • •

NOTES

• • •

MAINTAINING

_____

_____

_____

_____

_____

_____

_____

_____

_____

_____

_____

_____

_____

 _____

_____

_____

_____

_____

_____

• • •

• • •

DREAMING

It's not always possible to get everything you want in a home, especially not at first. But that doesn't mean that it will always be impossible. It's good to have some dreams for your home, some possibilities for the future. What would you do if you had all the time and money in the world—or just a little more time or money? What changes would you make if you didn't need to consult with anyone else on decorating or layout? What would you add or how would you reconfigure things if you suddenly had all the space you could want, and what would you add if you had just a little more space than you currently do? Think about what your home might look like if you could have anything you wanted, and jot down some of those ideas—you never know what the future might hold.

On the following grids, sketch out your ideal layouts for any spaces you'd like to remodel . . .

Describe your ideal color scheme for each room. How close
are the color schemes of your rooms to the ideal? Is there any
way to get closer to the ideal?

Sometimes it's not possible to do a full renovation when things get worn out. Are there any little touches of luxury you might be able to add to your life that would sustain you until you can do a renovation, such as installing new doorknobs or cabinet pulls, or painting an accent wall?

What reorganizing project would make your home more functional in the future—changing where you keep your pots and pans, for instance, or constructing a built-in filing cabinet? Brainstorm some ways to make it happen.

What's the best way to store your files? If there's a lot of paper cluttering up your home, can you make a plan to photograph or scan some of it so that you can keep some records in online file storage and free up physical space in your home?

_____

_____

_____

_____

_____

_____

_____

_____

_____

_____

_____

_____

_____

_____

_____

_____

_____

_____

Do any of the rooms in your house feel tired or boring? Brainstorm ways of making the space more visually appealing—whether it's a different paint color, a few accent pillows, a new piece of furniture, a houseplant, a rug or carpet, new lighting, or something else.

Are there any fun-yet-useful DIY projects you've always wanted to do but have never found time for, like reupholstering your headboard, or making trivets out of old wine corks? Or do you have any longer-term, more ambitious dream projects, like building a treehouse in your backyard or making your own dining room table?

PROJECT	TIMELINE	NOTES

Make a list of some of the projects you'd love to work on, and then think about when you might be able to make some time for them—a ten-minute break from work? Early on a weekend morning? At night after dinner? If you put in a few minutes of work a day, or an hour or two a week, before you know it you'll have created something useful—and all your own.

PROJECT	TIMELINE	NOTES

• • •

• • •

NOTES

· · ·

DREAMING

• • •

NOTES

• • •

NOTES

. . .

DREAMING

• • •

• • •

• • •

• • •

• • •

NOTES

• • •

DREAMING

• • •

• • •

NOTES

• • •

. . .

· · ·

NOTES

• • •

• • •

· · ·

• • •

NOTES

_____

_____

_____

_____

_____

_____

_____

_____

_____

_____

_____

_____

_____

_____

_____

_____

_____

_____

_____

· · ·

• • •

• • •

. . .